MODERN KID PRESS

grateful ♥hearts

A MOTHER-CHILD GRATITUDE JOURNAL OF APPRECIATION, LOVE, AND JOY

SABRINA SOTO

Email us at modernkidpress@gmail.com for freebies!

Just title the email "Grateful Hearts"
And we will send some extra
surprises your way!

Grateful Hearts

This book
belongs to

_____

and

_____

gratitude FOSTERS **resilience, optimism,** AND A SENSE OF **fulfillment**

Hello!

Welcome to **Grateful Hearts**, my new mother-child gratitude journal. I have a deep appreciation for the power of gratitude and the profound impact it can have on one's life. As mom to my daughter Olivia, I seek to instill this invaluable mindset in her always, encouraging her to embrace gratitude as a fundamental part of her daily life.

This journal is designed for a mother (by womb or by heart) and child to sit side-by-side in a daily moment of gratitude. I believe that by practicing gratitude together, we can embark on a transformative journey of self-reflection and appreciation. We can celebrate blessings and joys in our lives and develop a heightened awareness of the beauty surrounding us.

I hope you will join me in recognizing the importance of cultivating a mindset of gratitude as it fosters resilience, optimism, and a sense of fulfillment. Don't worry if you've never done something like this before. It's never too early to begin!

By documenting our experiences, thoughts, and expressions of gratitude daily, Olivia and I deepen our connection, learn from one another, and establish a lasting tradition that enriches our lives for years to come.

Happy journaling,

Sabrina

START EACH DAY
WITH GRATITUDE
AND WATCH YOUR
LIFE TRANSFORM
INTO A
**beautiful
adventure**

Child

What superpower would you like to have?
How would you use it to bring joy to the world?

_____

_____

_____

_____

_____

_____

_____

_____

_____

_____

_____

_____

_____

_____

_____

Mother

What personal strength do you
possess that you are grateful for?

_____
_____
_____
_____
_____
_____
_____
_____
_____
_____
_____

Write 3 things you are grateful for:

1. _____

2. _____

3. _____

Child

Who are you grateful to have in your life?

_____

_____

_____

_____

_____

_____

_____

_____

_____

_____

_____

_____

_____

_____

_____

_____

Mother

What do you appreciate about your relationships,
and how can you work towards improving them?

_____

_____

_____

_____

_____

_____

_____

_____

_____

_____

_____

Write 3 things you are grateful for:

1. _____

2. _____

3. _____

Child

What was the best part of your day yesterday?

_____

_____

_____

_____

_____

_____

_____

_____

_____

_____

_____

_____

_____

_____

_____

_____

Mother

What are some positive changes that you could make in
your daily routine to improve your overall well-being?

_____

_____

_____

_____

_____

_____

_____

_____

_____

_____

_____

Write 3 things you are grateful for:

1. _____

2. _____

3. _____

Child

What item(s) in your home are you grateful to have?

_____

_____

_____

_____

_____

_____

_____

_____

_____

_____

_____

_____

_____

_____

_____

Mother

What do you appreciate about your home?

_____

_____

_____

_____

_____

_____

_____

_____

_____

_____

_____

Write 3 things you are grateful for:

1. _____

2. _____

3. _____

Child

What is one thing you have learned
recently that you are grateful for?

_____

_____

_____

_____

_____

_____

_____

_____

_____

_____

_____

_____

_____

_____

_____

_____

Mother

What are some negative habits or behaviors that you could eliminate from your life to improve your happiness?

_____

_____

_____

_____

_____

_____

_____

_____

_____

_____

_____

Write 3 things you are grateful for:

1. _____

2. _____

3. _____

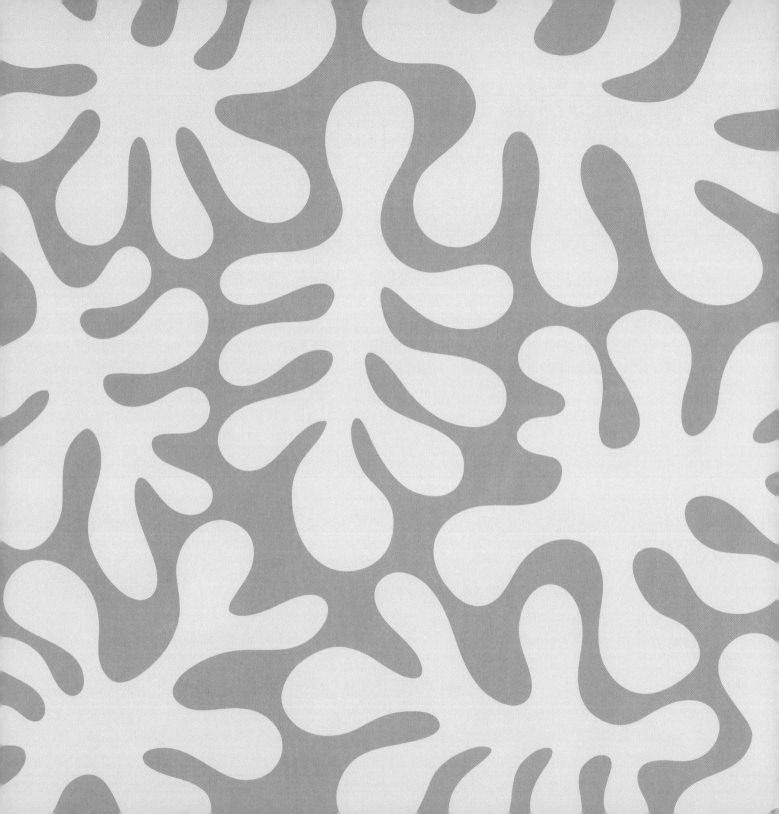

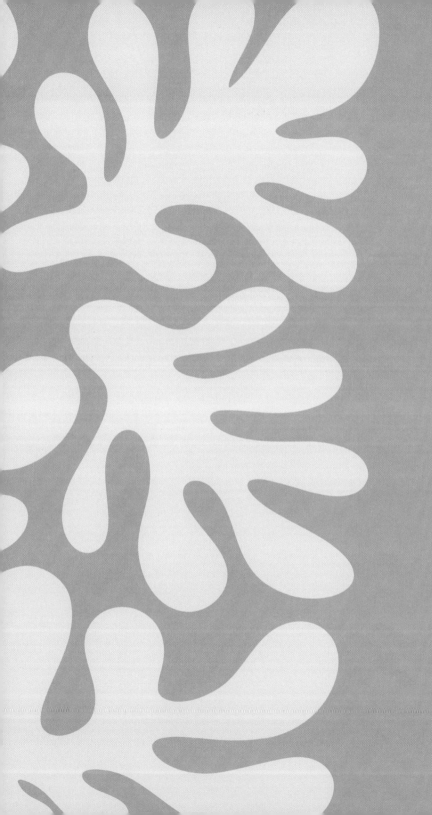

GRATITUDE IS NOT
JUST A FEELING,
**it's a way
of life**

Child

What is something nice someone did for you recently?

_____

_____

_____

_____

_____

_____

_____

_____

_____

_____

_____

_____

_____

_____

_____

Mother

Who are some people in your life who inspire you, and how can you learn from them to improve your own life?

_____

_____

_____

_____

_____

_____

_____

_____

_____

_____

_____

Write 3 things you are grateful for:

1. _____

2. _____

3. _____

Child

What is something you have
that makes you happy?

_____

_____

_____

_____

_____

_____

_____

_____

_____

_____

_____

_____

_____

_____

_____

_____

Mother

What do you appreciate about your spiritual life or beliefs,
and how can you deepen your connection to them?

_____

_____

_____

_____

_____

_____

_____

_____

_____

_____

_____

_____

Write 3 things you are grateful for:

1. _____

2. _____

3. _____

Child

What is a skill you have that you are grateful for?

_____

_____

_____

_____

_____

_____

_____

_____

_____

_____

_____

_____

_____

_____

_____

_____

Mother

What are some things you appreciate about your ability to love and be loved, and how can you strengthen your relationships with loved ones?

_____

_____

_____

_____

_____

_____

_____

_____

_____

_____

_____

_____

Write 3 things you are grateful for:

1. _____

2. _____

3. _____

Child

What is a special memory you have that you are grateful for?

_____

_____

_____

_____

_____

_____

_____

_____

_____

_____

_____

_____

_____

_____

_____

_____

_____

Mother

What do you appreciate about your mental health,
and how can you maintain or improve it?

_____

_____

_____

_____

_____

_____

_____

_____

_____

_____

_____

_____

Write 3 things you are grateful for:

1. _____

2. _____

3. _____

Child

What are you looking forward
to that you are grateful for?

_____

_____

_____

_____

_____

_____

_____

_____

_____

_____

_____

_____

_____

_____

_____

_____

Mother

What do you appreciate about your sense of purpose
or meaning in life, and how can you further pursue it?

_____
_____
_____
_____
_____
_____
_____
_____
_____
_____
_____

Write 3 things you are grateful for:

1. _____

2. _____

3. _____

GRATITUDE IS THE
FOUNDATION OF A
**peaceful
mind**

Child

Who is someone that makes
you feel happy and loved?

_____

_____

_____

_____

_____

_____

_____

_____

_____

_____

_____

_____

_____

_____

_____

_____

Mother

What do you appreciate about your physical health,
and how can you maintain or improve it?

_____
_____
_____
_____
_____
_____
_____
_____
_____
_____
_____
_____

Write 3 things you are grateful for:

1. _____

2. _____

3. _____

Child

What is your favorite thing
about your family?

_____

_____

_____

_____

_____

_____

_____

_____

_____

_____

_____

_____

_____

_____

_____

_____

Mother

What are some things that you can do today to show gratitude towards the people who support you?

_____
_____
_____
_____
_____
_____
_____
_____
_____
_____
_____
_____

Write 3 things you are grateful for:

1. _____

2. _____

3. _____

Child

What is a fun activity you are
grateful to be able to do?

_____

_____

_____

_____

_____

_____

_____

_____

_____

_____

_____

_____

_____

_____

_____

_____

Mother

What do you appreciate about your career or job, and how can you work towards achieving your goals?

_____
_____
_____
_____
_____
_____
_____
_____
_____
_____
_____

Write 3 things you are grateful for:

1. _____

2. _____

3. _____

Child

What is something that makes you laugh really hard?

_____

_____

_____

_____

_____

_____

_____

_____

_____

_____

_____

_____

_____

_____

_____

_____

Mother

What are some things that you appreciate about your community, and how can you become more involved and contribute to it?

_____

_____

_____

_____

_____

_____

_____

_____

_____

_____

_____

_____

Write 3 things you are grateful for:

1. _____

2. _____

3. _____

Child

What is something you have accomplished
recently that you are proud of?

_____

_____

_____

_____

_____

_____

_____

_____

_____

_____

_____

_____

_____

_____

_____

_____

_____

Mother

What are some limiting beliefs that you have about yourself, and how can you work to overcome them?

_____
_____
_____
_____
_____
_____
_____
_____
_____
_____
_____
_____

Write 3 things you are grateful for:

1. _____

2. _____

3. _____

A GRATEFUL
HEART IS A
**happy
heart**

Child

What is your favorite thing
about your school?

_____

_____

_____

_____

_____

_____

_____

_____

_____

_____

_____

_____

_____

_____

_____

_____

Mother

What do you appreciate about your education or personal growth, and how can you continue to learn and grow?

_____

_____

_____

_____

_____

_____

_____

_____

_____

_____

_____

_____

_____

Write 3 things you are grateful for:

1. _____

2. _____

3. _____

Child

What is your favorite thing about
the place where you live?

_____

_____

_____

_____

_____

_____

_____

_____

_____

_____

_____

_____

_____

_____

_____

_____

Mother

What do you appreciate about your hobbies or interests, and how can you make more time for them in your life?

_____
_____
_____
_____
_____
_____
_____
_____
_____
_____
_____
_____

Write 3 things you are grateful for:

1. _____

2. _____

3. _____

Child

What is your favorite thing about
the season we are in right now?

_____
_____
_____
_____
_____
_____
_____
_____
_____
_____
_____
_____
_____
_____
_____
_____
_____

Mother

What do you appreciate about your physical appearance,
and how can you embrace and enhance it?

_____

_____

_____

_____

_____

_____

_____

_____

_____

_____

_____

Write 3 things you are grateful for:

1. _____

2. _____

3. _____

Child

What are you grateful for that you may take for granted?

_____

_____

_____

_____

_____

_____

_____

_____

_____

_____

_____

_____

_____

_____

_____

_____

_____

_____

Mother

What are three things that you would
like to improve in your life, and why?

_____
_____
_____
_____
_____
_____
_____
_____
_____
_____
_____
_____

Write 3 things you are grateful for:

1. _____

2. _____

3. _____

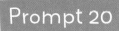

Child

What is something you have that you know
others may not have that you are grateful for?

_____

_____

_____

_____

_____

_____

_____

_____

_____

_____

_____

_____

_____

_____

_____

_____

_____

Mother

What do you appreciate about your financial situation, and how can you work towards achieving your financial goals?

_____

_____

_____

_____

_____

_____

_____

_____

_____

_____

_____

_____

Write 3 things you are grateful for:

1. _____

2. _____

3. _____

GRATITUDE IS
THE BRIDGE THAT
CONNECTS US TO
**abundance
and joy**

Child

What is something that you are
grateful to have learned recently?

_____

_____

_____

_____

_____

_____

_____

_____

_____

_____

_____

_____

_____

_____

_____

_____

Mother

What are some things that you can do today
to show gratitude towards yourself?

_____

_____

_____

_____

_____

_____

_____

_____

_____

_____

_____

Write 3 things you are grateful for:

1. _____

2. _____

3. _____

Child

What is a new friendship that you are grateful for?

_____

_____

_____

_____

_____

_____

_____

_____

_____

_____

_____

_____

_____

_____

_____

_____

_____

_____

Mother

What do you appreciate about your ability to forgive,
and how can you use it to improve your relationships?

_____

_____

_____

_____

_____

_____

_____

_____

_____

_____

_____

_____

Write 3 things you are grateful for:

1. _____

2. _____

3. _____

Child

What is something you are
grateful for about your body?

_____

_____

_____

_____

_____

_____

_____

_____

_____

_____

_____

_____

_____

_____

_____

_____

Mother

What do you appreciate about your ability to listen and communicate, and how can you use it to better connect with others?

_____

_____

_____

_____

_____

_____

_____

_____

_____

_____

_____

_____

Write 3 things you are grateful for:

1. _____

2. _____

3. _____

Child

What is something you are grateful for about your mind?

_____

_____

_____

_____

_____

_____

_____

_____

_____

_____

_____

_____

_____

_____

_____

_____

Mother

What are some positive habits or behaviors that
you could cultivate to improve your happiness?

_____

_____

_____

_____

_____

_____

_____

_____

_____

_____

_____

_____

Write 3 things you are grateful for:

1. _____

2. _____

3. _____

Child

What is something you are
grateful for about your heart?

_____

_____

_____

_____

_____

_____

_____

_____

_____

_____

_____

_____

_____

_____

_____

_____

_____

Mother

What do you appreciate about your sense of humor,
and how can you use it to bring joy to others?

_____

_____

_____

_____

_____

_____

_____

_____

_____

_____

_____

_____

Write 3 things you are grateful for:

1. _____

2. _____

3. _____

GRATITUDE IS THE
memory of
the heart

Child

What is something you are
grateful for about nature?

_____

_____

_____

_____

_____

_____

_____

_____

_____

_____

_____

_____

_____

_____

_____

_____

Mother

What do you appreciate about your creativity, and how can you use it to bring more joy and fulfillment to your life?

_____

_____

_____

_____

_____

_____

_____

_____

_____

_____

_____

Write 3 things you are grateful for:

1. _____

2. _____

3. _____

Child

What is something you are
grateful for about your community?

_____

_____

_____

_____

_____

_____

_____

_____

_____

_____

_____

_____

_____

_____

_____

_____

Mother

What do you appreciate about your ability to empathize with others, and how can you use it to support and help others?

_____
_____
_____
_____
_____
_____
_____
_____
_____
_____
_____
_____

Write 3 things you are grateful for:

1. _____

2. _____

3. _____

Child

What is something you are
grateful for about your country?

_____

_____

_____

_____

_____

_____

_____

_____

_____

_____

_____

_____

_____

_____

_____

_____

Mother

What do you appreciate about your ability to problem-solve, and how can you use them to overcome challenges in your life?

_____
_____
_____
_____
_____
_____
_____
_____
_____
_____
_____

Write 3 things you are grateful for:

1. _____

2. _____

3. _____

Child

What is something you are grateful for about the world?

_____

_____

_____

_____

_____

_____

_____

_____

_____

_____

_____

_____

_____

_____

_____

_____

Mother

What do you appreciate about your sense of adventure, and how can you use it to try new things and explore new opportunities?

_____

_____

_____

_____

_____

_____

_____

_____

_____

_____

_____

_____

Write 3 things you are grateful for:

1. _____

2. _____

3. _____

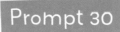

Child

What is your favorite thing about your friends?

_____

_____

_____

_____

_____

_____

_____

_____

_____

_____

_____

_____

_____

_____

_____

_____

_____

_____

Mother

What do you appreciate about your sense of gratitude, and how can you use it to cultivate more joy and happiness in your life?

_____

_____

_____

_____

_____

_____

_____

_____

_____

_____

_____

_____

Write 3 things you are grateful for:

1. _____

2. _____

3. _____

About Sabrina Soto

Sabrina Soto is an interior designer, television personality, and author known for her expertise in home decor and design. She has gained prominence through her appearances on various television shows, including HGTV's "The High Low Project," "Get It Sold," and TLC's "Trading Spaces." Sabrina's design style is characterized by a fusion of modern and eclectic elements, creating vibrant and welcoming spaces that reflect the personalities and lifestyles of her clients. With her warm and approachable demeanor, she has become a popular figure in the home improvement and design industry. Through her work, Sabrina Soto has inspired countless individuals to embrace their creativity, transform their living spaces, and create homes that truly reflect their unique identities.

Currently living in Los Angeles, Sabrina juggles being a mom to Olivia, designing, consulting and filming. When not working on a project, she treats her friends and family to her second passion of cooking.